ISAAC ASIMOV'S
Library of the Universe

Rockets, Probes, and Satellites

by Isaac Asimov

Gareth Stevens Publishing
Milwaukee

The reproduction rights to all photographs and
illustrations in this book are controlled by the
individuals or institutions credited on page 32 and
may not be reproduced without their permission.

Library of Congress Cataloging-in-Publication Data

Asimov, Isaac, 1920-
  Rockets, probes, and satellites.

  (Isaac Asimov's library of the universe)
  Bibliography: p.
  Includes index.
  Summary: Examines the origins, functions, uses, and discoveries of rockets,
space probes, and satellites.
  1. Rocketry—Juvenile literature. 2. Artificial satellites—Juvenile
literature. 3. Space probes—Juvenile literature. [1. Rocketry. 2. Artificial
satellites. 3. Space probes] I. Title. II. Series: Asimov, Isaac, 1920-
Library of the Universe.
TL793.A825   1988   629.43'5   87-42639
ISBN 1-55532-391-X
ISBN 1-55532-366-9 (lib. bdg.)

A Gareth Stevens Children's Books edition. Edited, designed, and produced by

Gareth Stevens, Inc.
7317 West Green Tree Road   Milwaukee, Wisconsin 53223, USA

Cover photography © NASA

Designer: Laurie Shock
Picture research: Kathy Keller
Artwork commissioning: Kathy Keller and Laurie Shock
Project editor: Mark Sachner
Technical adviser and consulting editor: Greg Walz-Chojnacki

2 3 4 5 6 7 8 9 9 93 92 91 90 89 88

CONTENTS

Introduction

The Universe we live in is an enormously large place. Only in the last 50 years or so have we found out how large it really is.

It's only natural that we would want to understand the place we live in. In the last 50 years we have developed new instruments that have told us far more about the Universe than could possibly have been imagined when I was young.

Nowadays, we have seen planets up close. We have learned about quasars and pulsars, about black holes and supernovas. We have learned amazing facts about how the Universe may have come into being and how it may end. Nothing can be more astonishing and more interesting.

❦ ❦

One of the ways we have learned new things about the Universe is by the use of rockets. With rockets we have sent artificial satellites around Earth and probes to distant planets. We have even sent men and women into space, and 12 men so far have walked on the Moon. Without rockets, a great deal of what we now know about outer space would have remained mysterious. In this book, then, let's find out something about rockets, probes, and satellites.

The Origins of Rocketry

It could happen in the Americas, Europe, Asia, Australasia, or Africa. In any of these places, a rocket could be propelling a satellite through the Earth's atmosphere and into outer space. But where did rocketry begin? Was it in the United States? The Soviet Union?

Actually, rockets were invented in the country with the world's fourth largest space program — behind the US, Soviet Union, and European Space Agency. It happened in the 1200s, long before there was a US or Soviet Union. It was the Chinese who first packed gunpowder into a cardboard cylinder. When they lit the gunpowder by a fuse, gases were formed that pushed out backward, and the rocket moved forward. In 1687, an English scientist, Isaac Newton, explained the science of how the rocket moved forward when the gunpowder exploded. His explanation is known as the law of action and reaction.

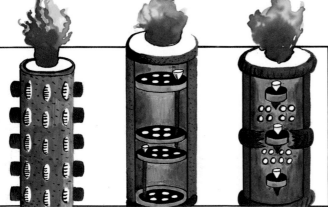

©Laurie Shock 1988

Top: As these three 17th-century models show, all rockets are basically tubes.

Bottom right: An arsenal of rockets. These were used during the 13th century by Mongolians in wars against people from Japan, the Middle East, and Europe.

©Laurie Shock 1988

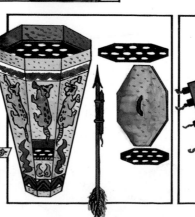

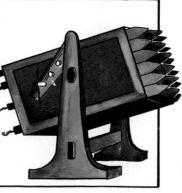

Bottom left: A 17th-century Chinese rocket-arrow launcher. Shown here are the launcher, the rocket-arrow, and the various parts of the launcher. Each hole in the launcher held a rocket, and all could be fired at once.

In the early 1800s rockets were sometimes used to carry explosives in war. When Francis Scott Key wrote about "the rockets' red glare" in "The Star-Spangled Banner," these are the rockets he meant.

Top: China, 1984: A rocket successfully clears its launch pad, lifting a Chinese communications satellite into orbit.

Bottom: A rocket showing Newton's law of action and reaction. Upper: Liquid hydrogen and oxygen are sent to the combustion chamber, where they mix and ignite. Lower: The hot gases created by the ignition rush out of the nozzle (action), causing the rocket to move in the opposite direction (reaction).

Oberg Archives

Konstantin Eduardovich Tsiolkovsky, space pioneer.
He was the first to suggest many ideas that have
since become reality, including using liquid oxygen
and hydrogen to fuel high-speed rockets and using
artificial satellites and jet-propelled rockets in space.

The Pioneers of Modern Rocketry

Later on, by the 20th century, some scientists had begun to
realize that rockets were one way that objects could be pushed
through space. The first to do so in detail, beginning in 1903,
was a Russian, K.E. Tsiolkovsky. An American, Robert H. Goddard,
continued that work and, in 1926, he sent up the first rocket of a
new kind. Instead of gunpowder, he used gasoline and liquid oxygen.
For the next 15 years, Goddard kept designing and shooting off
better and better rockets. Of course, working on rockets that would
be big enough and powerful enough to use in space has never
stopped people from using them to carry weapons on Earth.

Another space pioneer, Robert H. Goddard: At his blackboard at Clark University in Worcester, Massachusetts, 1924 (below); and with the world's first liquid-fueled rocket, 1926 (above). This picture was probably taken in Goddard's back yard, where he generally shot off his rockets.

Smithsonian Institution

Birth of the Space Age

During World War II, the Germans developed rockets big enough and powerful enough to bomb London in 1944. After the war, both the United States and the Soviet Union began to develop large rockets for exploring space.

On October 4, 1957, a Soviet rocket sent up Earth's first artificial satellite. It was called Sputnik 1. Sputnik 1 moved so quickly that it remained in orbit about the Earth in an egg-shaped orbit 142-588 miles (228-947 km) high. Sputnik 1 circled the Earth every 90 minutes.

On January 31, 1958, the United States launched its own satellite, Explorer 1. What we call the Space Age had begun!

The ugly aftermath of the German bombing of London in World War II.

Left: In Russian, <u>sputnik</u> means "traveling companion." Sputnik 2 became Earth's second artificial traveling companion on November 3, 1957. One of its three sections housed the dog Laika, the first living being in space. She died before all the tests on her were finished.

Right: On October 4, 1957, Sputnik 1 blasted off from the Soviet Union and, as shown here, took its place in orbit around Earth.

Catch some satellite-shine!

Some artificial satellites are visible from Earth. When is the best time to see them? Actually, we can often see them at night, when they look like bright stars moving across the sky. We can see them because they reflect sunlight — just like a planet or our own natural satellite, the Moon.

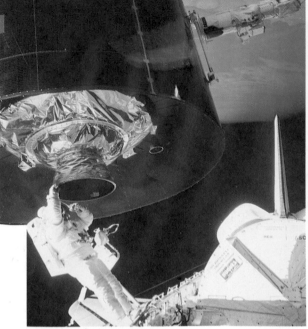

Discovery astronauts Joe Allen and Dale Gardner move a stranded Palapa B-2 communications satellite into Discovery's cargo bay for its trip back to Earth (1984).

With Earth gleaming behind him, astronaut William F. Fisher works outside his shuttle on a "captured" communications satellite that will soon be returned to orbit (1985).

A night space shuttle launch. Shuttles might one day carry astronauts and equipment back and forth between Earth and large, permanent space stations.

Rockets and Satellites at Work

Satellites do much more than circle the Earth. They do many kinds of work. Since 1958, for example, many communications satellites have been sent into orbit. They can receive radio waves from one place, make them stronger, and send them to a completely different place. Today, television programs and telephone calls can be sent easily from continent to continent. We can see and hear things as they happen on the other side of our planet. Since 1981, we have had space shuttles — rocket ships that can be used over and over again. Shuttles can carry satellites into space and place these satellites in orbit.

Joe Allen has just rescued another stranded satellite and is wrapping up his duties high above Earth (1984).

Left to right: Canadian, Japanese, and Indonesian communications satellites just seconds after liftoff at Cape Canaveral. Once in orbit, the Indonesian Palapa-1 instantly hooked up 3,000 islands and 120 million Indonesians to telephone, TV, and radio.

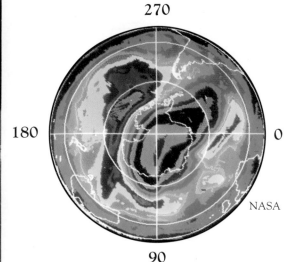

NASA

Tiros 8, a weather satellite sent into orbit in 1963 to take and instantly transmit pictures of cloud patterns to ground stations on Earth.

270

180

0

90

NASA

A map using information sent back to Earth by Nimbus 7. This satellite keeps track of the ozone layer that protects Earth from some of the Sun's ultraviolet rays. The dark violet area shows a deep hole in the ozone over Antarctica. This hole warns us to be careful about the chemicals we put into our atmosphere.

Forecasting the Weather

Special weather satellites began to be sent up in 1960. While orbiting the Earth, they take photographs of Earth and send them down in the form of radio waves. When these radio waves are received on Earth, weather people can create the satellite pictures we see on the news each night. For the first time in history, we can see the clouds covering all of the Earth and watch how they move. This makes it much easier to predict the weather. For example, we can see large circular cloud formations that make up hurricanes. Before 1960, we couldn't always tell when a hurricane might hit. Now people can board up their homes and leave before it comes. Countless lives have been saved in this way.

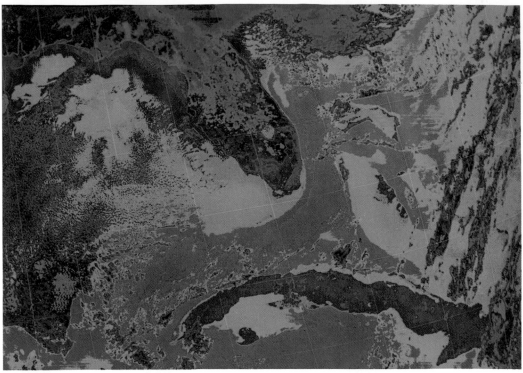

This is a thermal (heat) map of Florida and Cuba taken by
the Nimbus 5 weather satellite. Cuba and the water along
the Gulf Coast (red) show up as warmer than Florida and
Mexico's Yucatan Peninsula (blue and green). In Florida,
Lake Okeechobee (yellow) and the Everglades (red) also
show up as warmer than other parts of Florida.

Thunderclouds whirl over
the Amazon Basin, Brazil.
This photo was taken from
Apollo 9 in 1969.

A dramatic Earth-sky shot of Hurricane
Gladys (1968), as seen from the Apollo 7
spacecraft, 99 miles (160 km) over the
Gulf of Mexico.

Reading Earth from Space

Satellites can also take pictures of Earth itself when clouds aren't in the way. This makes it possible to make very exact maps. And now a ship at sea can receive messages from satellites that help the ship calculate its position exactly.

Satellite pictures can also tell the condition of forests and croplands. They can pinpoint trouble areas and the spread of plant diseases. The ocean, and schools of fish in it, can be studied, too.

Many satellites do this work from a geostationary orbit. A geostationary satellite must be at least 22,300 miles (35,680 km) high. A satellite at this height can orbit at the same speed as Earth's rotation. Therefore, it could stay over one area of the Earth at all times. Geostationary satellites may be used for telecommunications, weather forecasting, or even spying. By moving up into space, we learn a great deal more about our own Earth than we ever knew before. Now we can read Earth from outer space!

A Landsat view from New York City to Norfolk, Virginia. Landsat's altitude was 560 miles (902 km), and with the help of an atlas you can spot many familiar cities and rivers.

NASA

A spectacular ESA shot –
Italy's "boot" and neighboring
Europe and North Africa.

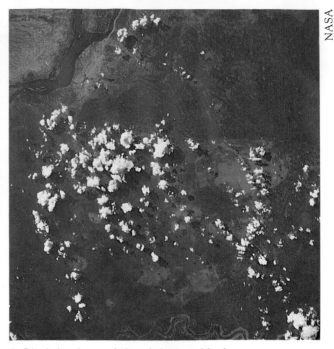

A Skylab view of the Arizona-Utah
border area showing the Colorado
River and Grand Canyon.

High above Florida, the Space
Shuttle Challenger, a tiny dot
atop its plume of steam, heads
toward its second mission (1983).

The ups and downs
of spying by satellite

*A spy satellite might take a picture of
Earth from 100 miles (160 km) up. This
picture would be so clear that you could
tell whether a coin on the ground was
heads or tails! Some spy satellites are
even higher. In 1987, a geostationary
US spy satellite over Lebanon spotted
a group of missing hostages being
moved from one building to another.
The satellite's recorders and cameras
could listen in on walkie-talkie radio
conversations, make out the faces of
some of the hostages, and figure out
what some of the buildings were made
of. All this could be done at night or
through thick clouds and from a height
of at least 22,300 miles (35,680 km)!
So the next time you're completely
alone, think about spy satellites and
the amazing things they can see —
and even hear — from outer space.*

An assortment of satellites and probes, shown here in an artist's rendition leaving their home base, Earth, behind. Clockwise, from upper right: Voyager (US), Mariner 6 or 7 (US), Ulysses (European Space Agency-ESA), Pioneer (US), Hubble Space Telescope (US), Vega (USSR), and Galileo (US).

Visiting the Moon and Other Worlds

So satellites tell us many things about Earth. What else can they do? They can move outward and skim by other worlds, or actually land on them. They are then called probes. The nearest other world is Earth's Moon, which is only about a quarter-million (250,000) miles (400,000 km) away. In 1959, a Lunar probe skimmed by the Moon and sent back pictures of the far side. It was the first time human beings had ever seen the far side, for it is always turned away from Earth. With each Lunar shot, the probes came closer and closer to the Moon. Finally, on July 20, 1969, a probe piloted by humans landed on the Moon. Neil Armstrong became the first human being who ever stepped onto another world.

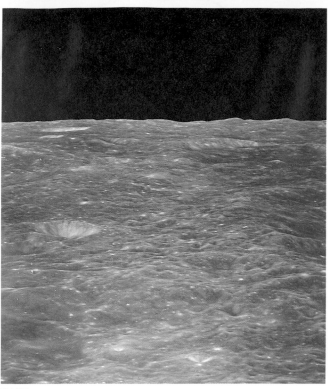

NASA

Upper left: The far side of the Moon as photographed by the Apollo 8 astronauts in December, 1968. This view shows at least two ways that the far side differs from the near side. It has fewer spectacular craters and a landscape brightly lit by a Sun that is sometimes directly overhead.

NASA

Upper right: This view of the Moon's far side covers an area about 20 miles (32 km) on each side.

NASA

Apollo 11 Commander Neil Armstrong in his Lunar Module (July, 1969) on the Lunar surface. Lunar life seems to agree with him!

NASA

A view of the near Lunar surface from Apollo 8. The large crater with the floor markings is about 20 miles (32 km) across.

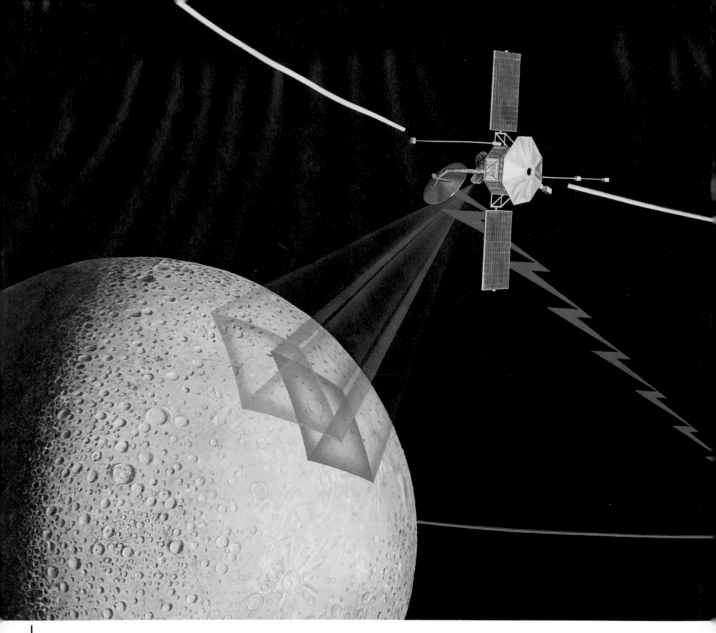

Mariner 10 to Mercury

No human being has yet gone farther than the Moon, but unpiloted probes have gone much farther. In 1974 and 1975, a Mercury probe, called Mariner 10, skimmed by the planet Mercury several times. At one time, it came within 168 miles (270 km) of the surface. It took photographs as it went by. Mercury is the planet that is closest to the Sun. Before Mariner 10, people could see it only as a tiny circle. The probe showed us most of Mercury's surface in full detail. It looked very much like our Moon, with many craters on it.

This NASA picture illustrates
Mariner 10 swooping past
the sunlit side of Mercury and
transmitting pictures back to Earth.

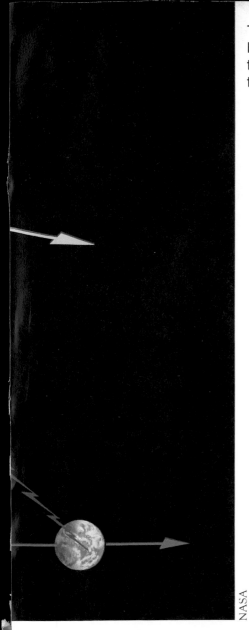

NASA

Moon-like Mercury. It's the
smallest planet in the Solar
system, and it has no moons
of its own. This striking photo
was taken by Mariner from
about 125,000 miles (200,000
km) above the planet.

NASA

NASA

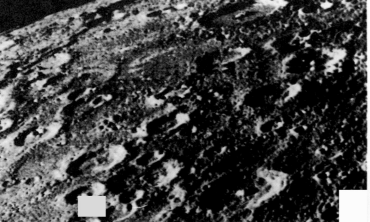

With no atmosphere to burn up
asteroids that come too close, tiny
Mercury has taken quite a beating in
its billions of years in the Solar
system.

Visits to Venus

People have wondered for years what it would be like to visit Venus. It is between Earth and Mercury, and so it is closer to the Sun than we are. It has a thick permanent cloud cover that hides the surface from us. Venus probes began to pass Venus in 1962. They showed that its thick atmosphere held in the heat, so that Venus was even hotter than Mercury.

Radio waves of the kind used in radar can penetrate clouds, and some probes bounced such waves off the surface of Venus. In this way maps could be made of the surface with radio waves doing the job of light waves. Probes even sent cameras down through the hot, thick atmosphere of Venus. These cameras were able to take photographs on the surface before they were ruined by the heat and pressure.

Probing the Venusian cloud cover

Venus is almost the same size as Earth, and it is a little closer to the Sun. Because it has a thick cloud layer, people thought till the 1950s that it might have a huge ocean that might even be full of life. However, probes have shown that Venus is extremely hot — hot enough to melt lead. It is therefore completely dry. The clouds contain water and also sulfuric acid. What's more, it turned out that Venus turns very slowly. It makes only one turn in 243 days, and it turns in the wrong direction — at least from the way we see things! Earth and almost all the worlds in the Solar system turn from west to east. Venus turns from east to west.

A gas balloon, dropped by a Soviet Vega probe, floating freely in the heavy atmosphere of Venus. The balloon transmitted data about the atmosphere, temperatures, and winds of Venus.

©Mark Maxwell

Viking to Mars

Could there be life on Mars? We know more about this question now than ever before. Mars is the nearest planet to us as we move away from the Sun. During the early 1900s, some astronomers thought they saw thin, straight lines, called canals, on the surface of Mars. They thought intelligent beings might exist there. Beginning in 1965, Mars probes passed by the planet and sent back photographs. We found out that there were no canals. There were, instead, canyons, dead volcanoes, many craters, and a very thin atmosphere. In 1976, two probes, Viking 1 and Viking 2, landed on Martian soil. These probes tested the soil to see if simple life might exist on Mars. It seems that none does.

NASA

NASA

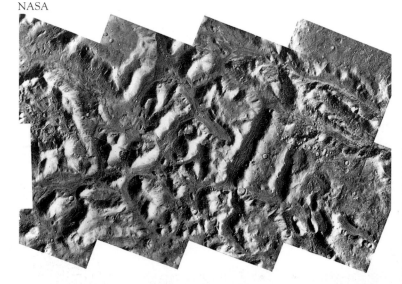

These two sets of photos were made from pictures taken by the Viking probes. The Viking 1 picture (below) reveals a mixture of smooth and cratered Martian landscapes. The Viking 2 picture (above) shows a section of the northern polar ice cap where wind may have driven bits of ice and soil into a streaked pattern.

A full-size working model of the Viking lander. It is seven feet (2.1 m) high and weighs about a ton. It has many special features, including a soil sampler that extends out in front and two camera "eyes" that stick up just behind the sampler.

NASA

NASA

It's about 15 minutes before sunset, and the shadows are getting longer across a stretch of the Martian landscape. This color photo was taken by the Viking 1 lander, and you can actually see part of the lander in the picture.

Probing Mars — many questions remain

Mars doesn't have any canals, but there are markings on it that look like dried-up rivers. Could it be that some time long in the past, there was lots of water on Mars? If so, what happened to it? And during the time when there might have been water on Mars, did life develop? If so, are there any traces of it left? Mars is the planet most like Earth, and anything we can do to understand it better might help us understand Earth better, too.

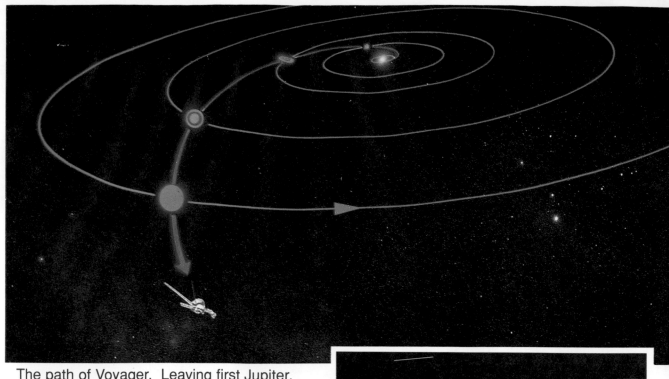

The path of Voyager. Leaving first Jupiter, then Saturn, Uranus, and Neptune behind, Voyager heads for the stars.

Voyager 1 was in the right place at the right time when it took this spectacular picture of Io, one of Jupiter's large moons. A huge volcanic explosion has occurred, and it appears just over Io's horizon. Give that probe a prize!

NASA

Pioneer and Voyager — To Jupiter, Saturn, and Uranus

So much for our neighbors. What lies beyond? Several probes, named Pioneer and Voyager, have gone past Mars to the farthest reaches of our Solar system. Beginning in 1973, they explored the giant planets that circle the Sun at great distances. They skimmed by Jupiter, the largest, and studied its large natural satellites, or moons. They found live volcanoes on one moon, Io, and a world-wide glacier on another moon, Europa. Beyond Jupiter, they sent back close-up pictures of Saturn and its enormous rings. The rings turned out to be full of complicated detail. Beyond Saturn, in 1986, photographs were sent back of still more distant Uranus.

©Julian Baum 1987

A picture of Saturn and its magnificent rings. Voyager 2 took this photo from a distance of about 2.1 million miles (3.4 million km).

NASA

NSSDC

NASA

Voyager clearly shows the flat, solid-ice surface of Europa, another of Jupiter's large moons.

"The Sounds of Earth" – a record sent into the cosmos aboard Voyager 2. Its messages to any extraterrestrials who care to listen include two hours of music, plus pictures and a greeting from US President Jimmy Carter expressed in computer language.

Probing Jupiter, a giant among giants

Jupiter is the largest of the planets. It is 318 times as massive as Earth. It has more than twice the mass of all the other planets put together. It also has many natural satellites, or moons. Four of them are quite large. One moon, Ganymede, is the largest of all satellites in the Solar system. In fact, it is actually larger than the planet Mercury! Jupiter's next largest satellite is Callisto. Both Callisto and Ganymede are made up largely of ice and are covered with craters. Jupiter also has a thin ring that was first discovered by probes, but it is nothing like the enormous rings of Saturn.

Future Missions

And what of the future? Voyager 2, which photographed Uranus, will soon pass by Neptune, the most distant of the large planets. We know very little about Neptune. Eventually, a probe called Galileo will drop a package containing instruments on Jupiter. On its way to Jupiter, Galileo will also fly by Venus and some asteroids and even tell us more about Earth. For the first time, we will have information about the inner regions of a giant planet's atmosphere. Closer to home, we are planning to build space stations between Earth and the Moon. We can then build other structures, and maybe even permanent living quarters, on the Moon itself.

Galileo's package of scientific goodies wafts silently through Jupiter's atmosphere.

Satellites and probes have given us eyes deep in space. Will we leave it at that? It's not very likely. Many think we are getting closer and closer to the day when we colonize other worlds.

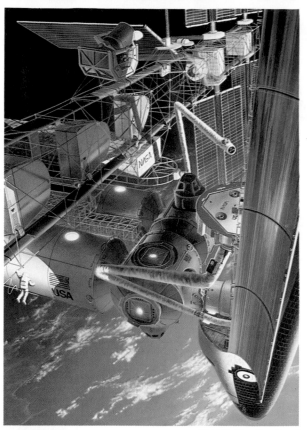

NASA (Pat Rawlings)

Space stations – our stepping stones to the cosmos? The day may come when space shuttles will routinely ferry astronauts and equipment to and from space stations high above Earth. These stations would give us a base for observing the cosmos and for sending probes and people to other parts of the Solar system.

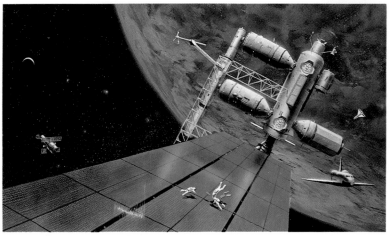

©Ron Miller

An enormous space station looms over both the shuttle craft approaching it and the Hubble Space Telescope nearby.

Probing Saturn's Titan — still lots to find out

Saturn has a moon that is almost as large as Jupiter's moon Ganymede. It is named Titan, and it is the second largest natural satellite in the Solar system. Since Titan is nearly twice as far from the Sun as Ganymede is, it is much colder. A cold world is better able to hold an atmosphere than a warmer one is. Titan has a thick atmosphere — it is the only satellite known to have one. Probes have shown that the atmosphere contains gases known as nitrogen and methane. The atmosphere is misty, though, and we can't see Titan's surface. What lies on Titan underneath the atmosphere? We don't know.

27

Fact File: Rockets, Probes, and Satellites

Here is one look at the sky above. It gives you an idea of the incredible assortment of satellites that the nations of Earth have sent up. These satellites give us new ways of understanding our Earth and space, predicting the weather, communicating with one another, performing technological experiments, and even spying on one another.

Dozens of nations have launched satellites into space. But few actually have their own launch sites, and thus many must use the launch pads of a very few. The chart below gives information about some major launch sites, along with some clues to help you find them on a map. One interesting note: The Earth spins eastward with greater velocity, or speed, closer to the Equator. So a rocket launched near the Equator would get a greater natural boost into space from the planet's rotation. Is it any wonder that most countries try to build their launch sites close to the Equator, which is at 0° latitude?

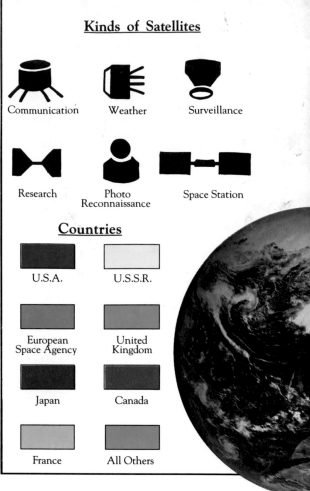

Kinds of Satellites

Communication   Weather   Surveillance

Research   Photo Reconnaissance   Space Station

Countries

U.S.A.   U.S.S.R.

European Space Agency   United Kingdom

Japan   Canada

France   All Others

Where We Send Them Up: Some of the World's Major Launch Sites

Country:	USA	USSR	FRANCE (European Space Agency)
Site:	Kennedy Space Center	Tyuratam-Baikonur	Kourou
Location:	Cape Canaveral, Florida	Soviet Kazakhstan	French Guiana
Latitude & Longitude:	28.5° north 81° west	46° north 63.5° east	5.3° north 52.5° west
Comments:*	Chief US site. Called Cape Kennedy 1963-1973, then renamed Canaveral.	Soviet "Canaveral." All piloted USSR craft launched here.	The major space center for European Space Agency(ESA) program.

*"Comments" from information in Luigi Broglio et. al., *Quest for Space* (New York: Crescent Books, 1987), pp. 14-19.

A Skyful of Satellites

| 90-300 mi
145-483 km | 300-630 mi
483-1,014 km | 630-1,250 mi
1,014-2,013 km | 1,250-3,100 mi
2,013-4,991 km | 3,100-6,200 mi
4,991-9,982 km | 6,200-13,700 mi
9,982-22,057 km | 13,700-21,750 mi
22,057-35,018 km | 21,750-22,370 mi
35,018-36,016 km |

©Kathy Keller and Laurie Shock

ITALY	JAPAN	CHINA	INDIA
San Marco	Kagoshima-Uchinoura	Shuang-ch'eng-tzu ("East Wind")	SHAR-Sriharikota
Formosa (Ungama) Bay, Kenya	Kyushu Island, Japan	Jiayuguan, China	Sriharikota Island, India
2.9° south 41° east	31° north 130.4° east	40.25° north 99.5° east	13.5° north 81.3° east
Launch site of US Uhuru satellite — 1st discovery of possible black hole.	Built in 1963. Launches University of Tokyo scientific satellites only.	Run by team of technicians trained in both US and USSR.	First launching in 1971. Also one of four Indian space study centers.

More Books About Rockets, Probes, and Satellites

Here are more books about rocketry and space exploration. If you are interested in them, check your library or bookstore.

Artificial Satellites. Bendick (Franklin Watts)
Colonies in Orbit. Knight (Morrow)
How Do You Go to the Bathroom in Space? Pogue (TOR Books)
Out to Launch: Model Rockets. Olney (Lothrop, Lee & Shepard)
Space Machines. Ciupik & Seevers (Raintree)
Voyager: The Story of a Space Mission. Poynter & Lane (Atheneum)

Places to Visit

You can explore the Universe – including the places to which rockets, probes, and satellites are launched – without leaving Earth. Here are some museums and centers where you can find many different kinds of space exhibits.

Ontario Science Centre
Toronto, Ontario

The Space and Rocket Center
Huntsville, Alabama

NASA John F. Kennedy Space Center
Kennedy Space Center, Florida

NASA Lyndon B. Johnson Space Center
Houston, Texas

For More Information About Rockets, Probes, and Satellites

Here are some people you can write away to for more information about rockets, probes, and satellites. Be sure to tell them exactly what you want to know about. And include your full name and address so they can write back.

**For information about
   rocketry and propulsion:**
NASA Lewis Research Center
Educational Services Office
21000 Brookpark Road
Cleveland, Ohio 44135

About weather satellites:
National Climatic Center
Satellite Data Service Division
World Weather Building, Room 100
Washington, DC 20233

About planetary missions:
NASA Jet Propulsion Laboratory
Public Affairs 180-201
4800 Oak Grove Drive
Pasadena, California 91109

For agricultural photos and data:
Western Aerial Photography Lab
Department of Agriculture
2505 Parley's Way
Salt Lake City, Utah 84109

**For Landsat, Skylab, and
   NASA photos of Earth:**
EROS Data Center
10th and Dakota Avenue
Sioux Falls, South Dakota 57198

**About earth-orbiting observation
   satellites (photos and data):**
National Satellite Science Data Center
NASA Goddard Space Flight Center,
   Code 601.4
Greenbelt, Maryland 20771

Glossary

asteroids: very small planets made of rock or metal. There are thousands of them in our Solar system, and most of them orbit the Sun between Mars and Jupiter. But some show up elsewhere in the Solar system — some as meteoroids and some possibly as "captured" moons of planets, such as Mars.

astronomers: people who study the many bodies of the Universe.

atmosphere: the gases that surround a planet.

communications satellites: satellites that receive radio waves from one location, make them stronger, and send them to any place on Earth. This makes sending phone calls and television shows over great distances a simple matter.

Explorer 1: the first US artificial satellite, launched on January 31, 1958.

geostationary satellite: a satellite that is in orbit above the Earth's Equator at an altitude of 22,300 miles (35,680 km) and at a speed matching Earth's rotation. A geostationary satellite can stay over one area of Earth at all times.

Lunar probe: a spacecraft mission to the Moon. In 1959 a Lunar probe photographed the far side of the Moon for the first time.

Mariner 10: a probe that passed by and photographed Mercury in 1974 and 1975.

Pioneer and Voyager: probes that are exploring the farthest reaches of our Solar system.

probes: spacecraft that travel in space, photographing celestial bodies and even landing on some of them.

Solar system: the Sun, planets, and all the other bodies that orbit the Sun.

satellite: a smaller body orbiting a larger body. The Moon is Earth's <u>natural</u> satellite. Sputnik 1 and 2 were Earth's first <u>artificial</u> satellites.

space shuttles: rocket ships that can be used over and over again since they return to Earth after completing their missions.

space stations: artificial bodies in space in which humans live and work, often for months.

Sputnik: the first artificial satellite to orbit Earth. The Soviets launched Sputnik on October 4, 1957.

Viking 1: the first successful probe to land on Mars (1976).

weather satellites: satellites that take pictures of Earth and send them back as radio signals. These help weather forecasters predict weather all over the world.

Index

The publishers wish to thank the following for permission to reproduce copyright material: front cover, pp. 7 (upper), 10 (all), 11 (all), 12 (all), 13 (all), 14, 15 (top right, lower), 17 (all), 18-19 (all), 22-23 (all), 24 (lower), 25 (upper, lower right), 27 (by Pat Rawlings) (upper), courtesy of NASA; p. 4 (all), © Laurie Shock 1988; p. 5 (upper), Xin Hua News Agency; p. 5 (lower), © Sally Bensusen 1987; pp. 6, 9 (right), Oberg Archives; pp. 7 (lower), 9 (left), Smithsonian Institution; p. 15 (upper left), European Space Agency; p. 16, © Lynette Cook; p. 21 © Mark Maxwell; pp. 24 (upper), 26 , © Julian Baum; p. 25 (lower left), National Space Science Data Center; p. 27, © Ron Miller; pp. 28-29, © Kathy Keller and Laurie Shock.